Microwave

ROZ DENNY

MEREHURST

LONDON

Contents

Managing Editor: Janet Illsley
Photographer: Alan Newnham
Designer: Sue Storey
Food Stylist: Lyn Rutherford
Photographic Stylist: Maria Jacques
Typeset by Angel Graphics
Colour separation by J. Film Process Limited, Thailand
Printed in Italy by New Interlitho S.p.A.

Published 1990 by Merehurst Ltd,
Ferry House, 51/57 Lacy Rd, Putney, London SW15 1PR

© Merehurst Ltd

ISBN: 1 85391 135 6

NOTES

All spoon measures are level: 1 tablespoon = 15ml spoon;
1 teaspoon = 5ml spoon.
Use fresh herbs and freshly ground black pepper unless
otherwise stated.

Introduction

It wasn't until I found myself on a self-catering holiday without a microwave oven that I realised just how much it had become an integral part of my cooking. It is invaluable for all sorts of quick family dishes. I also noticed that without my faithful old micro-friend, there seemed to be an awful lot more pots and pans to wash up!

However, a microwave oven has its limitations, just as a conventional cooker does. I will not try to artificially brown food in a microwave, nor will I spend time taking dishes in and out of the microwave to stir if they can be cooked more easily in a conventional oven or on the hob.

I have therefore created this collection of recipes to bring out the best in a microwave. There are a few pointers, though, that I would like to draw your attention to.

These dishes have been tested in a 650 watt oven with a turntable and no browning unit. If your oven has higher or lower wattage, adjust times accordingly. Check your instruction book for times and power levels. If you do not have a turntable, then you must turn the food during cooking. My timings are intended as a guide only. Always undercook at first – it is easy to increase timings.

Use microwave-proof dishes and covers. This won't necessarily mean buying special microwave equipment: many of your existing glass, china and earthenware containers will be fine as long as they contain no metal. If using cling film or plastic wrap, make sure it is microwave-quality and always pierce a few times before using.

I hope you enjoy using these recipes and cooking by microwave as much as I do.

Ro Danny

Summer Soup

This is a lovely, fresh-tasting minestrone-style soup – ideal served as a light summer lunch with rolls, which can be heated briefly in the microwave.

1 onion, sliced
1 clove garlic, crushed
2 tablespoons olive oil
250g (8oz) courgettes (zucchini),
* thinly sliced*
400g (14oz) can chopped
* tomatoes*
940ml (1½ pints/3¾ cups)
* chicken or vegetable stock*

3 tablespoons dry white wine or
* cider (optional)*
2 tablespoons chopped basil
60g (2oz/⅓ cup) small dried
* pasta shapes or thin macaroni*
salt and pepper
TO SERVE:
basil leaves
freshly grated Parmesan cheese

1 Put the onion, garlic and oil in a deep bowl. Cover and cook on HIGH for 3 minutes. Add the courgettes (zucchini), stir, cover and cook for 2 minutes.

2 Stir in the tomatoes, stock, wine or cider if using, basil and pasta, and season well. Cover and cook, stirring once or twice during cooking, for 10 minutes or until the pasta is *al dente* – just cooked.

3 Check seasoning and serve, garnished with basil. Sprinkle with Parmesan cheese to taste. *Serves 4-6.*

Avocado & Bacon Soup

If you enjoy avocados, you might like to try this South American dish. It has a deliciously delicate flavour and can be eaten hot or cold.

4 rashers lean streaky bacon,
  rinds removed, chopped
2 tablespoons olive oil
1 onion, very finely chopped
940ml (1½ pints/3¾ cups)
  hot chicken or vegetable stock
2 medium ripe avocados
155ml (5 fl oz/⅔ cup) single
  (light) cream

salt and pepper to taste
2 tablespoons dry sherry
juice of ½ lemon
TO GARNISH:
chopped chives
2-3 tablespoons double (thick)
  cream (optional)

1 Put the bacon and oil in a large microwave-proof jug and cook, uncovered, on HIGH for 3 minutes, stirring once. Remove the bacon with a slotted spoon and drain on absorbent kitchen paper.

2 Add the onion to the jug, stir, cover and cook for 5 minutes. Add the stock, cover and cook for 7 minutes or until boiling steadily.

3 Meanwhile, peel, halve and roughly chop the avocados, discarding stones. Put the avocado, cream and seasoning in a food processor or blender and blend to a purée. With the machine still running, slowly pour in the hot stock through the funnel and blend until smooth.

4 Return the soup to the jug and cook, uncovered, on HIGH just to reheat, about 3 minutes, stirring twice. The soup may look as if it is separating, but quickly turns smooth when stirred.

5 Stir in the sherry and lemon juice just before serving. Top each portion with bacon, chives, and a swirl of cream if desired. *Serves 4-6.*

VARIATION: If serving cold, omit step 4 and chill soup. Thin with extra cream or chilled stock if liked.

Chinese Chicken Soup

The Chinese are great soup eaters, although in China soup is usually served between courses. They always start with a good homemade stock – which is no trouble to make in a microwave.

STOCK:
1 small chicken, about 1 kg (2lb)
  plus gizzard if available, but
  not other giblets
2 spare-rib pork bones or small
  pork bone (optional)
1 large carrot, roughly chopped
1 stick celery, chopped
2.5cm (1 inch) piece fresh root
  (green) ginger, peeled and
  chopped
3 spring onions (green shallots),
  chopped
1 star anise
2 tablespoons light soy sauce
salt and pepper

SOUP:
2 thin carrots, peeled and very
  thinly sliced diagonally
2 spring onions (green shallots),
  sliced diagonally
90g (3oz) oyster mushrooms
  or large button mushrooms,
  sliced
3 tablespoons light soy sauce
3 tablespoons dry sherry
1 teaspoon sesame oil
1 bunch watercress, roughly
  chopped
TO GARNISH:
coriander sprigs

1 Put all the stock ingredients into a large deep bowl. Cover with at least 1.7 litres (3 pints/7½ cups) cold water. Cover the bowl with microwave-quality plastic wrap, pierced a few times. Cook on HIGH for 1 hour. Cool, strain, then chill. Remove the chicken breasts and shred finely; keep rest of the chicken for another dish. Discard the vegetables etc. When the stock is cold, skim off the fat.

2 Pour 1.2 litres (2 pints/5 cups) stock into a clean deep bowl. (Use leftover stock for other dishes.) Cover and reheat on HIGH until boiling, about 12 minutes. Add carrots and spring onions (shallots) and cook for 2 minutes.

3 Add the shredded chicken with the mushrooms, soy sauce, sherry and sesame oil. Stir well and cook for 2 minutes. Check the seasoning, stir in the watercress and serve hot, garnished with coriander. *Serves 4-6.*

Mussel & Haddock Chowder

A bowl of this wholesome soup is a meal in itself. Serve with bread or crackers. For added luxury, add a spoonful or two of dry sherry just before serving.

500g (1lb) mussels, scrubbed
375g (12oz) smoked haddock or
  cod (not dyed)
315ml (10fl oz/1¼ cups) milk
625ml (1 pint/2½ cups) fish
  stock or water
1 large bay leaf
salt and pepper
good pinch of saffron threads or
  ½ teaspoon turmeric
1 onion, thinly sliced

1 medium potato, peeled and
  chopped
2 leeks, sliced
60g (2oz) butter, cut into pieces
2 tomatoes, skinned and
  chopped
3 tablespoons single (light)
  cream
2 tablespoons chopped parsley
  (optional)

1 Clean the mussels, discarding any that are open.

2 Put the haddock or cod into a deep dish with the milk, stock or water, bay leaf and seasoning. Cover and cook on HIGH for 5 minutes. Allow to stand for 5 minutes then strain off the liquor, stir in the saffron or turmeric and reserve. Skin and flake the fish.

3 Put the onion, potato, leeks and butter into a deep bowl. Cover and cook on HIGH for 5 minutes. Add the liquor and tomatoes. Cover and cook for 10 minutes or until the potatoes are soft and pulpy.

4 Add the mussels, stir well and cook, uncovered, for 5 minutes or until they all open. Discard any that remain closed.

5 Stir in the cream and flaked fish, and reheat on HIGH for 2 minutes, then sprinkle with chopped parsley, if desired. Serve hot. *Serves 4.*

Marbled Vegetable Terrine

This starter not only looks attractive, it tastes so refreshing. Vegetable terrines are popular alternatives to rich pâtés and are ideal if you are entertaining vegetarians. You will need three separate bowls to make this.

500g (1lb) spinach leaves, washed
500g (1lb) carrots, grated
500g (1lb) celeriac, grated
90g (3oz/1½ cups) fresh white breadcrumbs
155ml (5 fl oz/⅔ cup) whipping cream or thick Greek yogurt

3 eggs
salt and pepper
¼ teaspoon grated nutmeg
finely grated rind of ½ orange or 1 small lemon
2 teaspoons lemon juice
TO GARNISH:
parsley or coriander sprigs

1 Pat spinach leaves dry with a clean tea towel, then shred finely. Put in a large bowl, squashing down well, and add 2 tablespoons water. Cover and cook on HIGH for 6 minutes or until tender. Drain well and return to bowl.

2 Put the carrots in another bowl with 3 tablespoons water, cover and cook on HIGH for 8-10 minutes until tender, stirring once during cooking. Put the celeriac in another bowl with 4 tablespoons water, cover and cook on HIGH for 8-10 minutes. Drain both vegetables and return to bowls.

3 Divide the breadcrumbs and cream or yogurt equally between the vegetables. Add an egg to each and season well. Flavour the spinach with nutmeg, the carrots with orange or lemon rind and the celeriac with lemon juice. Mix well.

4 Lightly grease a 1.7 litre (3 pint) microwave loaf dish and randomly spoon in the vegetable mixtures in alternate tablespoonfuls. Level the top. Cover with microwave-quality plastic wrap and pierce a few times. Stand the dish on an upturned plate and cook on MEDIUM for 25 minutes or until the centre is just firm to touch. Stand for 5 minutes before turning out. Serve warm or chilled, cut into slices and garnished with parsley or coriander sprigs. Serve with a pretty leaf salad. *Serves 6.*

Oeufs Florentines

This is ideal for a quick supper dish or starter. Eggs can be baked in a microwave as long as the yolks are pierced first so that they do not burst. Here the eggs nestle in a bed of spinach, mixed with garlicky cream cheese.

1 small onion, chopped
2 tablespoons olive or
   sunflower oil
500g (1lb) spinach leaves,
   washed, trimmed and
   shredded coarsely
salt and pepper

50g (2oz) garlic cream cheese,
   softened
good pinch of ground cumin
4 eggs
45g (1½oz) Gruyere cheese, cut
   into strips
parsley sprigs to garnish

1 Put the onion and oil in a large microwave-proof bowl. Cover and cook on HIGH for 3 minutes. Add the spinach, pressing down well. Season, toss well, cover and cook on HIGH for 3 minutes. Stir, re-cover and cook for another 2 minutes.

2 Turn into a colander to drain off excess liquid, then return to the bowl and mix in the garlic cheese and cumin; season well.

3 Put the spinach in a shallow dish. Indent four 'wells' in the spinach, with the back of a tablespoon, and break an egg into each. Season the eggs and pierce each yolk once.

4 Cook on HIGH for 3-5 minutes, depending on how well you like your eggs cooked. Arrange the cheese on top of the eggs, return to the microwave and cook on HIGH for 20 seconds, just to melt the cheese. Serve immediately, garnished with parsley and accompanied by toast triangles. *Serves 2 or 4.*

Ginger Soy Prawn Satays

It is quick and easy to cook satay in a microwave and the little pieces of food stay nice and moist. You can thread the prawns in advance, ready for quick cooking just before you sit down to eat. It's fascinating to watch them cook – they turn a lovely shade of pink before your very eyes!

24 large raw oriental prawns
3 spring onions (green shallot),
  chopped
2.5cm (1 inch) cube fresh root
  (green) ginger, peeled and
  grated
1 clove garlic, crushed
3 tablespoons naturally brewed
  soy sauce
1 tablespoon sesame oil

2 tablespoons tomato ketchup
3 tablespoons dry sherry
1 tablespoon chopped coriander
salt and pepper
TO SERVE:
1 head curly endive (frisée),
  shredded
½ cucumber, shredded
1-2 teaspoons sesame seeds
juice of 1 lime or ½ lemon

1 Remove the heads from the prawns, peel off the legs and scales, but leave on the tails; devein if necessary.
2 Put all the remaining ingredients into a large polythene bag and shake to mix. Add the prawns and rub well to coat. Chill and leave to marinate for 2 hours or so.
3 Skewer the prawns on 8 bamboo satay sticks, three at a time, alternating tails. Arrange on a large dinner plate like the spokes of a wheel. Trim the sticks with kitchen scissors if they are too long.
4 Cook on HIGH for 2 minutes, then turn the sticks so that the other ends are pointing to the middle. Cook for another minute. Serve hot, as soon as possible. Garnish with a little salad of curly endive (frisée), cucumber and sesame seeds, dressed with a light sprinkling of fresh lime or lemon juice. *Serves 4 or 8.*

Salade Tiède

The idea of tossing a fresh, crisp salad with a tasty, hot dressing has become very popular, and the hassle of making it is reduced if you heat everything in a microwave. This salad uses a deliciously rich dressing flavoured with bacon, mushrooms, honey and coarse-grain mustard. It is also good as a dressing for avocados, which look particularly stylish if you nestle each half in a radicchio leaf.

1 small radicchio, shredded
2 heads of chicory (witlof),
*   thinly sliced*
½ cucumber, finely sliced
½ iceberg lettuce, shredded
DRESSING:
3 rashers lean, streaky bacon,
*   rinds removed, chopped*
2 tablespoons walnut, olive or
*   sunflower oil*

125g (4oz) button mushrooms,
*   sliced*
1 tablespoon cider or
*   wine vinegar*
2 tablespoons coarse-grain
*   mustard*
1 teaspoon clear honey
salt and pepper
TO GARNISH:
basil leaves

1 Combine the prepared salad ingredients in a large bowl.

2 To make the dressing, put the bacon and oil in a medium bowl, stir well then cover and cook on HIGH for 2 minutes. Add the mushrooms, stir well, re-cover and cook for a further 2 minutes.

3 Stir in the vinegar, mustard, honey and seasoning. Pour the dressing over the salad and toss together well. Serve immediately, garnished with basil. *Serves 4.*

Tagliatelle with Smoked Fish

It's not quicker to cook pasta in a microwave, but it is more convenient, especially if you only want to cook a small amount. The sauce that accompanies this is creamy and quick to make, besides being a tasty way to eat more nourishing, healthy fish.

125g (4oz) dried tagliatelle
1 tablespoon olive oil
salt and pepper
3 tablespoons crème fraîche or
thick sour cream
1 tablespoon fresh snipped
chives or dill, or both

125g (4oz) smoked mackerel or
trout, skinned and flaked
3 teaspoons red lumpfish caviar
1 teaspoon poppy seeds
(optional)

1 Put the tagliatelle into a deep, large bowl and add 1 teaspoon salt. Pour over sufficient boiling water to cover completely. Stir well, cover with microwave-quality plastic wrap and pierce a few times. Cook on HIGH for 5 minutes then stand for 2 minutes. Drain, but leave slightly wet. Return to bowl.

2 Toss in the oil, seasoning, crème fraîche or sour cream, herbs and smoked mackerel or trout. Reheat on HIGH for 2 minutes.

3 Transfer to warmed serving plates and scatter the caviar over the top. Sprinkle with poppy seeds, if desired. Serve immediately. *Serves 2.*

Salmon with Lemony Lentils

Put fish and pulses together to make a well-balanced, healthy dish that tastes really good too. Serve this with some crusty French or Italian bread and, perhaps, a radicchio and chicory salad.

*185g (6oz/1 cup) continental
  lentils, ideally small
  Puy lentils
2 bay leaves
1 small onion, chopped
2 tablespoons olive oil
juice of 1 small lemon
2 tablespoons chopped parsley
salt and pepper*

*1 large leek, cut into
  julienne strips
1 carrot, cut into julienne strips
45g (1½oz) butter
4 salmon steaks or fillets, about
  125g (4oz) each
TO GARNISH:
lemon wedges
parsley sprigs*

1 Soak the lentils in cold water for 2 hours. Drain, cover with boiling water in the same bowl and add the bay leaves and onion. Cover with microwave-quality plastic wrap and pierce a few times. Cook on HIGH for 10 minutes, then reduce to MEDIUM and cook for 25 minutes.

2 Drain and remove bay leaves. Stir in the oil, lemon juice and parsley. Season to taste.

3 Put the leeks and carrots in a shallow casserole dish, season and add 3 tablespoons water. Dot with a third of the butter. Cover and cook on HIGH for 3 minutes.

4 Put the salmon on top of the vegetables. Dot with the remaining butter, season, cover and cook on HIGH for 3-5 minutes, depending on the thickness of the fillet or steak.

5 Serve each salmon portion on a bed of vegetables, with the pan juices spooned over and accompanied by the lentils. Garnish with lemon and parsley. *Serves 4.*

Sole & Spinach Turbans

One of the best uses of the microwave is to cook fish. It is quick, simple and delicious as the fish retains its shape and flavour well. This dish looks spectacular, but is really easy to prepare and cook. Serve the turbans with béarnaise or tomato sauce, green beans or broccoli, and rice if desired.

*2 whole lemon soles, about 500g
   (1lb) each, skinned and
   filleted
juice of ½ lemon
185g (6oz) frozen leaf spinach,
   thawed, squeezed dry
   and chopped
150g (5oz) ricotta, curd or
   cream cheese*

*125g (4oz) peeled prawns,
   thawed if frozen, chopped
30g (1oz) butter, melted
grated nutmeg
salt and pepper
TO SERVE:
1 quantity béarnaise sauce (page
   46), or tomato sauce (page 48)
whole cooked prawns*

1 Cut each sole fillet in half lengthwise so you have 8 thin fillets. Grease 4 ramekin dishes. Season the fillets and sprinkle with lemon juice. Curl 2 fillets round the inside of each ramekin.

2 Mix the spinach, cheese, prawns, butter, nutmeg and seasoning together in a bowl, then spoon into the centre of each dish. Flatten the tops. Cover each with greased microwave-quality plastic wrap and pierce a few times.

3 Cook on HIGH for 4 minutes. Allow to stand for 2 minutes then drain off the juices into a cup and reserve.

4 Unmould the turbans onto a serving dish and keep warm. To serve, add the reserved juices to the béarnaise or tomato sauce. Serve the sauce separately or poured around the turbans. Garnish with whole prawns. *Serves 2 or 4.*

Skate with Piquant Sauce

Skate wings always look dramatic on a plate. Skate is quite a meaty fish and as the bones are so evident it is easy to fillet. The Mediterranean tomato sauce for this dish is flavoursome and colourful and complements the taste and texture of the fish well.

4 skate wings, about 185g
  (6oz) each
1 tablespoon chopped marjoram
30g (1oz) butter
TOMATO SAUCE:
1 red pepper, cored and chopped
1 large onion, chopped
2 cloves garlic, crushed
2 tablespoons olive oil
400g (14oz) can chopped
  tomatoes

juice of 1 orange
grated rind of ½ orange
1 tablespoon dry sherry
salt and pepper
TO GARNISH:
2 tablespoons capers
1-2 tablespoons chopped parsley
parsley and marjoram sprigs

1 First, make the tomato sauce. Put the red pepper, onion, garlic and oil in a deep bowl. Cover and cook on HIGH for 6 minutes, stirring once.
2 Add the rest of the sauce ingredients, seasoning well. Cook uncovered on HIGH for 5 minutes, stirring once. If you prefer a smooth sauce, blend in a food processor until smooth; otherwise leave chunky. Keep warm.
3 Lay the skate wings on a large round plate, placing the thick bony points to the centre. Top with marjoram, butter and seasoning. Cover with another plate. Cook on HIGH for 4 minutes. Rearrange the wings on the plate to ensure even cooking and cook for a further 2 minutes. Add the cooking juices to the tomato sauce.
4 Serve the skate immediately with the sauce spooned over, and capers and parsley scattered on top. Garnish with herb sprigs to serve. *Serves 4.*

Two Fish in Creamy Cider Sauce

Fish tastes delicious in a fruity cider sauce, and here the colours of the two kinds of fish make an attractive dish to bring to the table. Serve with noodles, or rice flavoured with parsley.

1kg (2lb) salmon or sea trout, filleted and skinned, bones, skin and head reserved
1 small onion, chopped
1 bay leaf
2 carrots, 1 roughly chopped, 1 sliced diagonally
few parsley stalks
salt and pepper
30g (1oz) butter
2 medium leeks, sliced diagonally

2 tablespoons plain flour
155ml (5 fl oz/²/₃ cup) dry cider
2 teaspoons chopped dill
375g (12oz) smoked haddock or cod
3 tablespoons crème fraîche or thick sour cream
TO GARNISH:
parsley and dill sprigs

1 To make the stock, put the salmon skin, bones and head in a deep bowl with 470ml (¾ pint/2 cups) water, the onion, bay leaf, chopped carrot, parsley stalks and seasoning. Cover with microwave-quality plastic wrap, and pierce a few times. Cook on HIGH for 20 minutes, then strain and reserve.

2 Put the other carrot in another bowl with the butter. Cover and cook on HIGH for 2 minutes. Add the leeks and cook for 2 minutes. Stir in the flour then gradually work in the stock, cider and dill.

3 Cover and cook for 5 minutes, stirring twice until smooth. Add the fish, cut into bite-size pieces. Cover and cook for 5 minutes, until just firm, stirring once.

4 Mix in the crème fraiche or thick sour cream and cook for 1 minute to reheat. Check the seasoning and serve hot, garnished with parsley and dill. *Serves 4-6.*

Cajun Chicken Gumbo

This Cajun dish from Louisiana is tasty, filling and spicy. Omit the cayenne pepper for a milder version.

2 teaspoons paprika
1/2-1 teaspoon cayenne pepper
1 teaspoon garlic salt
1 teaspoon dried thyme
3 tablespoons sunflower oil
8 small chicken drumsticks,
  skinned
1 green pepper, cored and
  coarsely chopped
1 onion, coarsely chopped
2 sticks celery, sliced
2 cloves garlic, crushed
250g (8oz) okra, topped
  and halved

185g (6oz) smoked sausage or
  pepperoni, sliced
2 tablespoons flour
315ml (10 fl oz/1 1/4 cups)
  chicken stock
4 tablespoons ready-made
  tomato sauce
salt and pepper
TO SERVE:
green tops of 2 spring onions
  (green shallots), shredded
2 tablespoons chopped parsley

1 Mix the paprika, cayenne, garlic salt, thyme and 1 table-spoon of the oil in a polythene food bag. Add the chicken and rub the mixture well into the flesh. Leave to marinate for 30 minutes or more.

2 Lay the drumsticks on a large, lightly greased plate, bones inwards. Cook on HIGH for 5 minutes. Turn the drumsticks over but don't rearrange. Cook for a further 5 minutes or until the chicken is cooked, then allow to stand for 3 minutes. Drain the juices into a cup.

3 Put the green pepper, onion, celery, garlic and remaining oil into a large casserole. Cover and cook on HIGH for 5 minutes. Stir in the chicken juices, okra and sausage. Cover and cook for a further 3 minutes.

4 Stir in the flour, then add the stock and tomato sauce. Season to taste. Cover and cook for 3 minutes, stirring once. Add the chicken, mix well, cover and cook for 5 minutes.

5 Serve hot, sprinkled with spring onion (shallot) shreds and parsley, and accompanied by plain boiled rice. *Serves 4.*

'Stir-fry' Chinese Chicken

As with all Chinese dishes, it is a good idea to prepare everything first; the cooking takes very little time. Fermented black beans can be found in Oriental food stores, either dried or canned.

250g (8oz) skinned chicken breast, cut into strips
3 tablespoons light soy sauce
2 cloves garlic, crushed
2 tablespoons sunflower oil
2 teaspoons cornflour
155ml (5 fl oz/²/₃ cup) chicken stock or water
2 tablespoons dry sherry
1 teaspoon clear honey
2 medium carrots, thinly sliced diagonally
4 cm (1¹/₂ inch) cube fresh root (green) ginger, shredded

2 spring onions (green shallots), thinly sliced diagonally
125g (4oz) oyster or button mushrooms, sliced
125g (4oz) mange tout (snow peas), topped and halved
155g (5oz) baby corn, halved
2 teaspoons sesame oil
3 tablespoons fermented black beans, rinsed and drained
freshly ground black pepper

1 Put the chicken in a bowl with the soy sauce and garlic and leave to marinate for 10 minutes. Drain, reserving marinade. Heat half the oil in a large shallow casserole dish on HIGH for 1 minute. Add the chicken, stir, then cook for 2 minutes until firm.

2 Mix the cornflour with the stock or water, sherry, honey and reserved marinade, then add to the chicken. Cover and cook on HIGH for 2 minutes, stirring once, until thickened. Reserve.

3 Mix the remaining oil, the carrots, ginger and spring onions (shallots) in another dish. Cover and cook on HIGH for 3 minutes. Add the mushrooms, mange tout (snow peas), baby corn and sesame oil. Cover and cook for 2 minutes.

4 Mix the chicken and vegetables together. Stir in the black beans and reheat for 1 minute. Season with pepper only. Serve immediately with instant egg or rice noodles. *Serves 4.*

Moroccan Mince with Eggs

The aromatic cooking of Morocco can easily be adapted to our food styles. Here is a delicious variation of a family favourite which can be made with lamb or beef. The baked eggs add an extra creaminess, and when garnished with salad leaves, the whole dish looks very inviting.

2 tablespoons olive or
  sunflower oil
500g (1lb) lean minced beef
  or lamb
2 cloves garlic, crushed
1 onion, chopped
1 teaspoon ground cinnamon
1 teaspoon ground coriander
1 teaspoon ground ginger
a little grated nutmeg

400g (14oz) can chopped
  tomatoes
1 tablespoon tomato purée
  (paste)
1 teaspoon grated orange rind
salt and pepper
4 eggs
TO GARNISH:
salad leaves
coriander sprigs

1 Heat the oil in a large shallow casserole dish on HIGH for 1 minute. Add the mince, stirring well. Cook for a further 3 minutes.

2 Add the garlic, onion and spices, stirring well. Cover and cook for 3 minutes.

3 Stir in the tomatoes, tomato purée (paste), orange rind and seasoning. Cover and cook for 2 minutes. Make four 'wells' in the mince with the back of a tablespoon and crack an egg into each.

4 Pierce the yolks once, cover and cook for 3-4 minutes depending on how firm you like your eggs.

5 Garnish with salad leaves and coriander. Serve at once with plain boiled rice. *Serves 4.*

Browning Dish Brochettes

Lean, tender cuts of meat cook beautifully in the microwave, and there are no messy pans to wash afterwards. This recipe uses the browning dish to its full advantage – rump steak in a tasty marinade takes next to no time to cook. Serve with salad and crusty bread.

500g (1lb) rump steak, trimmed
2 small onions
1 tablespoon sunflower oil
MARINADE:
1 tablespoon soy sauce
1 tablespoon Worcestershire
  sauce
1 teaspoon coarse-grain
  mustard

1 teaspoon clear honey
salt and pepper
TO GARNISH
1 teaspoon sesame seeds
watercress sprigs
parsley sprigs

1 Cut the steak into 16 neat bite-size pieces. Cut the onions into wedges.
2 Mix the marinade ingredients together in a polythene food bag and add the meat. Seal the bag and rub the meat well to absorb the marinade. Chill for 1 hour or so.
3 Measure 4 wooden satay sticks to fit the bottom of the browning dish. Trim the ends if necessary. Skewer the meat and onion wedges alternately onto the sticks.
4 Heat the empty browning dish on HIGH for 4 minutes. Add the oil, swirl around, then place the satays on the dish, pressing them down well to brown on the hot surface. After 30 seconds or so, turn them over and cook on HIGH for 2-4 minutes, depending on how you like your steak cooked.
5 Arrange the satays on a serving dish. Pour over the juices and sprinkle with sesame seeds. Garnish with watercress and parsley sprigs to serve. *Serves 2 or 4.*

Lamb with Baby Vegetables

Very young, tender vegetables need only the lightest cooking. Team them up with new season's lamb and the result is a light fresh casserole, particularly good with a liberal garnish of fresh herbs. If you are a keen gardener-cook, this is the recipe for you!

2 tablespoons sunflower oil
500g (1lb) lean boned leg
 of lamb, cubed
250g (8oz) each baby carrots,
 turnips or parsnips and leeks,
 prepared and halved if
 necessary
125g (4oz) button (baby) onions,
 peeled
155ml (5fl oz/²⁄₃ cup) dry
 white wine

2 teaspoons cornflour
315ml (10 fl oz/1¼ cups)
 lamb stock
2 tablespoons cream or yogurt
salt and pepper
1 tablespoon each chopped
 parsley and snipped chives
2 sprigs each thyme and
 marjoram, stripped from
 stalks

1 Lightly oil a large casserole with the sunflower oil and arrange the lamb on the base in a single layer. Cook on HIGH for 3 minutes. Turn the meat over, return to the microwave and cook for 2 minutes. Remove the meat with a slotted spoon and set aside.
2 Add all the vegetables to the casserole, stir, cover and cook on HIGH for 3 minutes, stirring once. Add the wine, cover and cook for 2 minutes.
3 Blend the cornflour with the stock, then stir into the casserole. Cover and cook for 2 minutes, until thickened. Return the meat to the casserole, pour in the cream or yogurt, season and stir well. Cover and cook for 3 minutes.
4 Sprinkle with the herbs and serve hot with noodles or new potatoes. *Serves 4.*

Pork & Waterchestnut Balls

These make a very tasty supper dish. Meatballs cooked in the microwave keep their nice round shape and can be cooked almost without any oil. The spicy soy sauce in this recipe ensures they have a good appetising colour, too.

500g (1lb) lean minced pork
3 rashers lean streaky bacon,
  rinds removed, chopped
1 clove garlic, crushed
1 teaspoon sesame oil
1 tablespoon soy sauce
pinch of five-spice powder
125g (4oz) canned
  waterchestnuts, drained
  and chopped
salt and pepper
oil for greasing

SAUCE:
155ml (5 fl oz/²/₃ cup) water
1 tablespoon dry sherry
2 teaspoons cornflour
1 teaspoon sesame oil
2 tablespoons soy sauce
TO GARNISH:
2 spring onions (green shallots),
  shredded
coriander or parsley sprigs

1 To make the meatballs, mix together the pork, bacon, garlic, sesame oil, soy sauce, five-spice and waterchestnuts in a bowl, seasoning well. With wet hands, shape into 12 meatballs.

2 Lightly brush a shallow casserole dish with oil, add the meatballs and cook uncovered on HIGH for 5 minutes. Change the positions of the meatballs from sides to middle, and cook again for 3 minutes.

3 Mix all the sauce ingredients together in a bowl and strain in the juices from the meatballs. Cook on HIGH for 2 minutes, stir well and cook for a further 2 minutes until thickened.

4 Pour the sauce over the meatballs and sprinkle with shredded spring onion (shallot). Garnish with coriander or parsley. Serve with rice or noodles. *Serves 4.*

Big Bean & Barley Pot

This is a cross between a soup and a main course – great for week-ends, or to make in bulk and freeze. If the sausage is omitted, it is ideal for vegetarians too.

125g (4oz/²⁄₃ cup) black eye or
  haricot beans
125g (4oz/²⁄₃ cup) mung or
  aduki beans
90g (3oz) pearl barley
1.3 litres (2¹⁄₂ pints/6¹⁄₄ cups)
  boiling water
1 teaspoon dried mixed herbs
1 vegetable stock cube, crumbled
1 onion, chopped
2 sticks celery, sliced
2 medium potatoes, coarsely
  chopped

1 green pepper, halved, cored,
  and sliced
400g (14oz) can chopped
  tomatoes
1 tablespoon Worcestershire
  sauce
salt and pepper
125g (4oz) chorizo or pepperoni
  sausage, sliced (optional)
TO SERVE:
marjoram or parsley sprigs
grated Cheddar cheese

1 Soak the beans in boiling water to cover for 1 hour. Drain and put in a deep dish with the barley.

2 Add the measured boiling water. Cover with microwave-quality plastic wrap and pierce a few times. Cook on HIGH for 10 minutes. Add the herbs, stock cube, onion, celery, potatoes and green pepper. Stir well. Cover and cook for 10 minutes.

3 Add the tomatoes, Worcestershire sauce and seasoning. Cook on MEDIUM for 35 minutes. Stir in the sausage, if using, and cook on HIGH for 5 minutes.

4 Serve in bowls, garnished with herbs, and hand grated cheese separately. *Serves 4-6.*

Chick Pea & Parsnip Curry

This is a real vegetarian feast – wholesome, spicy and tasty. Serve the curry with accompaniments such as chutneys, tiny poppadams, chopped tomato and cucumber salad, naan bread and best basmati rice.

1 onion, chopped
1 green or red pepper, cored and
  chopped
2 cloves garlic, crushed
2.5cm (1 inch) cube fresh root
  (green) ginger, grated
1 fresh green chilli, seeded and
  chopped (optional)
250g (8oz) young parsnips, cut
  into chunks
30g (1oz) butter or ghee
2 tablespoons sunflower oil
2 teaspoons curry powder
1 teaspoon cornflour (optional)
315ml (10 fl oz/1¼ cups)
  vegetable stock or water

125g (4oz) green beans, topped
  and halved
125g (4oz) mushrooms,
  quartered
salt and pepper
432g (15oz) can chick peas,
  drained
30g (1oz) creamed coconut,
  chopped
TO SERVE:
coriander sprigs
155ml (5 fl oz/⅔ cup) thick-set
  natural yogurt
2 tablespoons toasted desiccated
  coconut (optional)

1 Put the onion, pepper, garlic, ginger, fresh chilli if using, parsnips, butter or ghee and oil in a deep dish. Cover and cook on HIGH for 4 minutes, stirring once.
2 Stir in the curry powder and cook for 1 minute. If using the cornflour, blend with the stock or water then add to the dish with the beans and mushrooms. Season well, cover and cook for 5 minutes, stirring once.
3 Add the chick peas and coconut, stirring. Cook on HIGH for 2 minutes.
4 Garnish with coriander to serve and, either top with the yogurt and toasted coconut, or serve separately. *Serves 4-6.*

Asparagus with Béarnaise Sauce

It is so easy to make a Hollandaise sauce in the microwave without curdling. I have added some tarragon to make a classic béarnaise – perfect with asparagus. Although the asparagus can be cooked whole in the microwave, you have to spend time turning the spears during cooking, so I find it easier to cut them into dainty pieces instead.

75g (12oz) asparagus spears,
  woody ends trimmed
BEARNAISE SAUCE:
125g (4oz) unsalted butter,
  cut into pieces
2 egg yolks
juice of ½ lemon
2 teaspoons wine vinegar
1 teaspoon smooth French or
  coarse-grain mustard

1 tablespoon chopped tarragon
salt and white pepper
TO GARNISH:
60g (2oz/½ cup) chopped
  walnuts or hazelnuts
  (optional)
tarragon sprigs

1 Cut the asparagus into bite-size lengths. Put the stalk pieces in a bowl with 315ml (10 fl oz/1¼ cups) boiling water. Season, cover and cook on HIGH for 2-4 minutes, depending on the thickness of the stalks. Stir, then add the asparagus tips, cover and cook for 2 minutes. Allow to stand for 2 minutes, then drain well and arrange on a dish.

2 To make the sauce, put the butter on a dish and cook for 1 minute on DEFROST. Set aside. In a medium bowl, whisk the egg yolks, lemon juice, wine vinegar, mustard, tarragon and seasoning.

3 Cook uncovered on HIGH for 30 seconds. Remove and whisk in the butter until smooth and creamy. Spoon the sauce over the asparagus and scatter with nuts, if liked. Garnish with tarragon to serve. *Serves 4.*

Mediterranean Salad

Normally, one needs a lot of oil to cook aubergines (eggplants) until they are softened. Cooked in the microwave, they need much less oil, yet they still have a sautéed flavour. Peppers, however, need conventional grilling to give them a nice smoky taste. Make this dish a day ahead to allow the flavours to mature.

1 medium aubergine (eggplant),
   cut into thick chunks
salt
2 red or yellow peppers
2 tablespoons extra virgin
   olive oil
TOMATO SAUCE:
1 tablespoon extra virgin
   olive oil
1 onion, chopped
2 cloves garlic, crushed

3 tablespoons dry white wine
   (optional)
1 teaspoon fennel seeds
400g (14oz) can chopped
   tomatoes
salt and pepper
TO SERVE:
coriander or parsley leaves
2-3 tablespoons freshly grated
   Parmesan cheese (optional)

1 Put the aubergine (eggplant) chunks in a colander and sprinkle lightly with salt. Leave to drain for 20 minutes over a bowl, then rinse well and pat dry.

2 Meanwhile, preheat the grill and grill the peppers, turning frequently until their skins blister. Wrap in a clean tea towel and leave for 10 minutes, then peel, deseed and slice.

3 Put the aubergine (eggplant) in a large bowl, add the oil and mix well. Cover and cook on HIGH for 3 minutes, stir, cover and cook for 2 minutes. Allow to stand while you make the sauce. Combine the aubergine (eggplant) and peppers.

4 Put the oil, onion and garlic in another bowl, cover and cook on HIGH for 3 minutes. Add the wine if using, fennel seeds, tomatoes and seasoning. Cook uncovered for 7 minutes on HIGH, stirring once.

5 Pour the sauce over the aubergines and peppers, allow to cool to room temperature and serve, garnished with herbs, and Parmesan if desired. *Serves 4.*

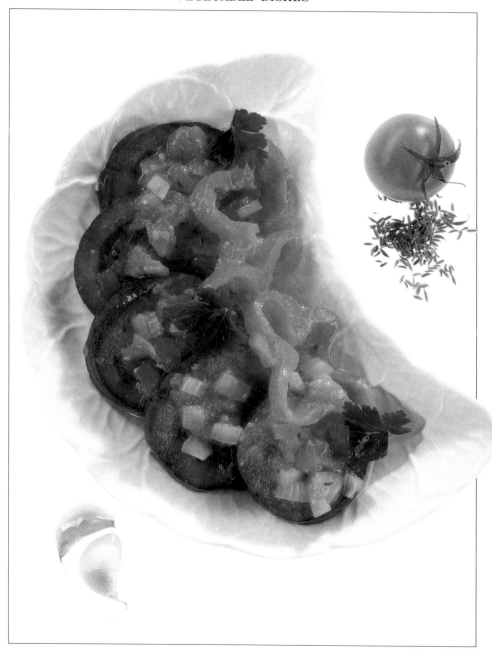

Baby Corn & Beans with Noodles

3 spring onions (green shallots),
  sliced diagonally
1 clove garlic, crushed
1cm (½ inch) cube fresh root
  (green) ginger, grated
2 tablespoons sunflower oil
185g (6oz) baby corn, halved
250g (8 oz) green beans, topped
  and halved
125g (4oz) button mushrooms,
  sliced

2-3 tablespoons light soy sauce
1 tablespoon dry sherry
2 teaspoons cornflour
pinch of sugar
6 tablespoons stock or water
125g (4oz) instant Chinese
  noodles
60g (2oz/⅓ cup) unsalted
  cashews
salt and pepper

1 Put the spring onions (shallots) garlic, ginger, oil, corn and beans into a large bowl. Stir well, cover and cook on HIGH for 3 minutes.
2 Add the mushrooms, cover and cook for 2 minutes. Mix the soy sauce, sherry, cornflour, sugar and stock together, then stir into the vegetables. Season and cook uncovered on HIGH for 2 minutes, until the sauce thickens.
3 Soak the noodles in boiling water for 4 minutes; drain. Mix with the vegetables and sprinkle with nuts. *Serves 4.*

Creamed Peas & Lettuce

1 small red onion, chopped
1 lettuce, shredded
30g (1oz) butter
500g (1lb) frozen garden peas
2 tablespoons chopped parsley

3-4 tablespoons thick sour
  cream
grated nutmeg
salt and pepper

1 Put the onion, lettuce and butter into a large bowl. Cover and cook on HIGH for 3 minutes, stirring once.
2 Add the peas, stir and cook for 5 minutes, stirring once.
3 Add the parsley, cream and nutmeg. Season with salt and pepper and serve immediately. *Serves 4.*

Risotto in Radicchio Cups

Proper Italian risotto is made with a special short-grain rice that cooks to a delicious creaminess. It can be made ahead, then reheated with more stock to moisten. Saffron strands and dried mushrooms are tasty additions; others include diced cooked chicken, peas, prawns, pinenuts and bacon.

15g (½oz) dried mushrooms –
  porcini or ceps (optional)
½ teaspoon saffron strands
  (optional)
785ml (1¼ pints/3 cups) light
  chicken or vegetable stock
1 onion, chopped
1 clove garlic, crushed
2 tablespoons olive oil
250g (8oz) risotto rice,
  preferably arborio grade
155ml (5 fl oz/⅔ cup) dry
  white wine

125g (4oz) button mushrooms,
  sliced
30g (1oz) butter
2 tablespoons chopped parsley
salt and pepper
TO SERVE:
4 large or 8 smaller radicchio
  leaves
30g (1oz) freshly grated
  Parmesan cheese

1 If using dried mushrooms and saffron, cut the mushrooms into tiny pieces and crush the saffron. Bring a little of the stock to the boil, add the mushrooms and saffron and leave to soak for about 10 minutes.

2 Meanwhile, put the onion, garlic and oil in a deep bowl. Cover and cook on HIGH for 5 minutes, stirring once.

3 Add the rice, stir and cook uncovered on HIGH for 2 minutes. Add the wine and mushrooms, stir well and cook for a further 2 minutes.

4 Pour in the stock, with the dried mushrooms and saffron if using. Season well. Cover and cook on HIGH for 10 minutes, stirring twice, until the rice is just tender and creamy.

5 Mix in the butter and parsley. Serve the risotto in radicchio leaves, sprinkled with Parmesan cheese. *Serves 4.*

Red Cabbage with Beer & Honey

1 onion, sliced
1 medium red cabbage,
  shredded
60g (2oz) butter
375ml (12 fl oz/1½ cups) stout
  or brown ale
1 tablespoon clear honey

1 tablespoon coarse-grain
  mustard
1 teaspoon cumin seeds
  (optional)
salt and pepper
TO GARNISH:
chopped parsley

1 Put all the ingredients into a large bowl, seasoning and stirring well. Cover and cook on HIGH for 10 minutes, stirring twice. Allow to stand for 5 minutes, then serve, sprinkled with parsley. *Serves 4-6.*

Broccoli & Cauliflower Mornay

1 medium cauliflower, broken
  into flowerets
250g (8oz) broccoli flowerets
SAUCE:
2 tablespoons flour
315ml (10 fl oz/1¼ cups) milk

30g (1oz) butter or margarine
salt and pepper
1 teaspoon caraway seeds
75g (3oz) mature Cheddar
  cheese, grated
1 teaspoon paprika pepper

1 Put the cauliflower and broccoli flowerets into a deep bowl. Add 315ml (10 fl oz/1¼ cups) salted boiling water. Cover and cook on HIGH for 5 minutes. If the stalks are still hard, cook for a further 2 minutes. Stand for 2 minutes, then drain, reserving 155ml (5 fl oz/⅔ cup) water. Arrange the flowerets in a dish.
2 Return the reserved water to the bowl. Add the flour, milk, butter or margarine, seasoning and caraway seeds if liked. Whisk together. Cook uncovered on HIGH for 2 minutes. Whisk again and cook for a further 2 minutes. Whisk once more and cook for 1 minute, then stir in the cheese. Pour the sauce over the vegetables and serve hot, sprinkled with paprika. *Serves 4.*

Fragrant Coconut Rice Pilau

Thai- and Indonesian-style food is deservedly gaining in popularity, as it mixes familiar and unusual ingredients in delectable combinations. This rice dish goes well with grilled or curried fish or chicken. Thai fish sauce is a wonderful 'season-all', similar to light soy sauce. It's worth tracking down in an Oriental food store.

155ml (5 fl oz/²⁄₃ cup) canned
coconut milk, or 2 tablespoons
  unsweetened desiccated
  coconut
250g (8oz/1¹⁄₂ cups) basmati
  rice, washed
1 stem fresh lemon grass, or
  1 teaspoon dried

4 cloves
¹⁄₄ nutmeg, grated
¹⁄₂ teaspoon ground cumin
2 tablespoons Thai fish sauce
salt and pepper
TO GARNISH:
lemon wedges
coriander sprigs

1 If canned coconut milk is not available, soak the desiccated coconut in 200ml (6¹⁄₂ fl oz/³⁄₄ cup) boiling water for 30 minutes. Strain into a jug. Squeeze the flesh, then discard. Make the coconut milk (canned or homemade) up to 560ml (18 fl oz/2¹⁄₄ cups) with water.
2 Pour the milk into a large bowl with the rice, lemon grass, spices, fish sauce and seasoning.
3 Cover and cook on HIGH for 12 minutes, stirring twice. Allow to stand for 5 minutes, then stir well to mix and to separate the grains.
4 Remove the whole spices, if liked, or warn your diners to watch out for them! Serve garnished with lemon wedges and coriander. *Serves 4-6.*

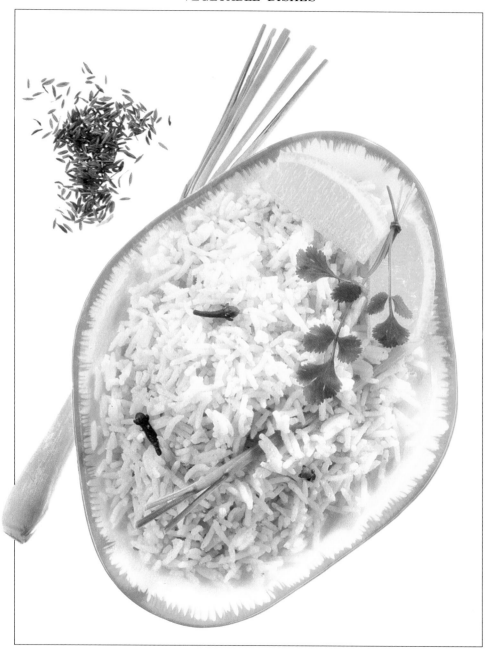

Ice Cream with Quick Sauces

The freezer and the microwave complement each other in many ways, but no better than in the provision of quick simple, delicious ice cream desserts. Don't forget that hard ice cream can be softened for easier serving by microwaving on DEFROST for 30 seconds or so, depending on the quantity. These two sauces can be quickly put together and reheated.

HOT CHOCOLATE FUDGE SAUCE:
60g (2oz) butter, cut into pieces
1 tablespoon cocoa powder
2 tablespoons soft brown sugar
155ml (5 fl oz/²/₃ cup)
  evaporated milk
pinch of salt
few drops of vanilla essence
60g (2oz) plain (dark) chocolate,
  in pieces, or dark chocolate
  cooking drops

BLACKCURRANT & MINT SAUCE:
250g (8oz) frozen blackcurrants,
  destalked
155ml (5 fl oz/²/₃ cup) water
2 tablespoons honey or caster
  sugar
1-2 tablespoons chopped mint
TO SERVE:
vanilla ice cream

1 To make the hot chocolate fudge sauce, put everything except the chocolate in a microwave jug. Cook on HIGH for 3 minutes, stirring once. Stir again and cook for 1 minute. Add the chocolate and stir until melted. If the chocolate has not completely melted return to the microwave and cook for 30 seconds or so; do not allow to boil. Cool to thicken slightly, before serving with ice cream.

2 To make the blackcurrant and mint sauce, put all the ingredients in a medium bowl and stir well. Cover and cook on HIGH for 3 minutes. Uncover and cook for a further 3-4 minutes until reduced and slightly pulpy. Cool for 5 minutes before spooning over ice cream. *Each sauce serves 4-6.*

Mango & Orange Sorbet Shells

These can be stored in the freezer, to be whipped out whenever you need an impressive dessert. Wrap them well in plastic freezer wrap or pack in a polythene freezer box. The mango chutney adds an extra spicy zing to the sorbet.

4 medium oranges, halved
60g (2oz/¼ cup) caster sugar
3 ripe mangoes, peeled, flesh cut
*   from stone and chopped*
1 teaspoon lemon juice

1½ tablespoons mango chutney,
*   chopped*
2 egg whites
TO GARNISH:
mint or borage leaves

1 Squeeze the juice from the oranges and pour into a jug. Make up to 125ml (4 fl oz/½ cup) with water if necessary. With a teaspoon, scrape out the pith and membranes from the orange shells.

2 Put the sugar and orange juice into a large bowl and cook on HIGH for 2 minutes. Stir, then add the mango chunks and lemon juice. Cover and cook on HIGH for 4 minutes. Stir in the chutney then leave until cold.

3 Blend the mixture to a puree in a food processor or blender. Pour into a rigid polythene freezer container and place in the freezer until just frozen, about 2 hours.

4 Remove from the freezer and beat well with a whisk to break down the ice crystals. Whisk the egg whites in a separate bowl until soft peaks form, then fold quickly and lightly into the frozen purée.

5 Spoon into the orange shells and return to the freezer for several hours until firm. If the sorbet is not to be eaten that day, cover the shells with plastic freezer wrap.

6 Allow to soften at room temperature for 20 minutes before serving, garnished with mint or borage leaves. *Serves 8.*

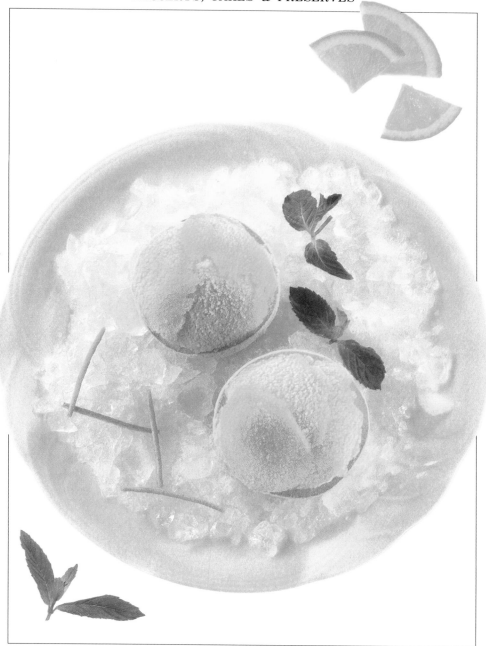

Orange & Grape Terrine

The microwave makes dissolving gelatine simple, so it becomes fun to experiment with fresh fruit jellies and mousses, confident that they will set.

6 large oranges
470ml (15 fl oz/1¾ cups) still
 white grape juice
4 teaspoons powdered gelatine
1 tablespoon clear honey
good pinch of ground cinnamon

500g (1lb) red or white seedless
 grapes, halved
SAUCE:
2-3 teaspoons arrowroot
470ml (15 fl oz/1¾ cups) orange
 juice

1 Line a 1kg (2lb) loaf tin with plastic wrap. (The tin does not have to be microwave-proof).
2 Cut the tops and bottoms off the oranges, then peel and remove the segments.
3 Put 2 tablespoons grape juice in a cup and sprinkle over the gelatine. Allow to soften, then cook on DEFROST for 1 minute. Remove and stir; there should be no granules left. If the mixture looks cloudy, let it stand for a minute or two before deciding whether it needs a few extra seconds in the microwave. Stir in the honey, remaining grape juice and cinnamon.
4 Pour a little of the liquid into the base of the tin and chill until set. Arrange the orange segments and grape halves in layers on top, pressing down well.
5 Pour the rest of the juice over slowly, so that it fills the spaces between the fruit. Tap the tin gently to make sure there are no air pockets. The terrine should be almost solid fruit, held together with jelly. Chill until quite firm.
6 Meanwhile, make the sauce. Mix the arrowroot with a little of the orange juice. Heat the rest in a microwave jug on HIGH for 5 minutes or until just boiling. Pour in the slaked arrowroot, stirring briskly. Cool.
7 Turn the terrine out onto a chilled plate and cut into thick slices. Arrange on individual plates, pour around the orange sauce and decorate with strawberries or grapes. *Serves 6.*

Spiced Rice Cream

If you thought rice pudding was nursery food, then you are in for a pleasant surprise with this dish. Cooking rice in a microwave is not only quicker, it gives the rice a light creaminess which is especially good when chilled. Serve the cream in dessert glasses with soft berry fruits or a salad of sliced kiwi, mango and pineapple. For an exotic touch, scatter over some pretty edible flowers or petals, such as roses, violets or borage.

90g (3oz/½ cup) pudding rice
2 tablespoons clear honey
1-2 tablespoons caster sugar
940ml (30 fl oz/3¾ cups) milk
1 large bay leaf

1 sprig fresh rosemary
6 whole cardamom pods
155ml (5 fl oz/⅔ cup) whipping
cream, whipped (optional)

1 Put all the ingredients, except the cream, into a deep microwave bowl. Cover with microwave-quality plastic wrap and pierce a few times. Cook on HIGH for 6 minutes. Uncover and stir. Cover and cook for a further 5 minutes or until the mixture comes to a boil.
2 Uncover, stir well and cook on DEFROST for 35-40 minutes, stirring two or three times; the rice will swell and the mixture reduce.
3 Allow to cool, then stir well and remove the herbs and cardamom pods. Serve at room temperature, or chill lightly and fold in the whipped cream. *Serves 4-6.*

Apple Salad in Wine Syrup

I prefer to use just one or two fruits in a fruit salad and to macerate them in the syrup. This makes a flavoursome and refreshing dessert. Apples poached in the microwave hold their shape well — no more slushy stewed apple!

3 tablespoons thin-shred
  maramalade
470ml (15 fl oz/1¾ cups) sweet
  dessert wine, e.g. Côtes de
  Bordeaux, Sauternes or
  Muscat de Beaumes de Venise
2 cinnamon sticks
4 Granny Smith apples, peeled
  and cored

2 tablespoons flaked almonds
TO SERVE:
315ml (10 fl oz/1¼ cups)
  whipping cream, lightly
  whipped
mint sprigs to decorate

1 Put the marmalade into a medium bowl and cook on HIGH for 2 minutes to soften. Stir, then gradually add the wine, stirring. Add the cinnamon and cook on HIGH for 10 minutes. Remove the cinnamon sticks.

2 Cut each apple into 6 rings. Arrange the apple slices in a shallow round dish, overlapping if necessary, and pour over the syrup.

3 Cook on HIGH for 3 minutes. Stir and cook for another 3 minutes. Cool, then chill lightly.

4 Meanwhile, spread the almonds on a plate and cook on HIGH for 4 minutes to brown lightly. Remove and cool.

5 Arrange the apples in individual serving dishes and spoon over the syrup. Scatter over the nuts and top with dollops of cream and mint sprigs. *Serves 4-6.*

Night & Day Mousse

Melting chocolate the traditional way in a bowl over a pan of simmering water is often a messy and risky business. In the microwave it becomes a very smooth operation!

125g (4oz) white chocolate,
* in pieces*
315ml (10 fl oz/1¼ cups) double
* (thick) cream*
4 eggs, separated
125g (4oz) plain (dark)
* chocolate, in pieces*
½ teaspoon instant coffee
* granules*

2 tablespoons water
1 tablespoon brandy or Tia
* Maria (optional)*
TO DECORATE:
30-60g (1-2oz) bar plain
* (dark) chocolate*

1 Put the white chocolate in a medium bowl with half the cream. Cover and cook on MEDIUM for 2 minutes or until the chocolate has melted. Stir well. Cover and cook again for 1 minute until just below boiling. Stir again until smooth. Do not let the mixture boil or it will 'sieze' and go into hard lumps. Beat in 2 egg yolks.
2 In another bowl, melt the plain (dark) chocolate with the remaining cream in the same way, then beat in the other 2 egg yolks.
3 Mix the coffee and water in a cup and cook on HIGH for 30 seconds. Stir to dissolve. Beat into the dark chocolate mixture with the brandy or liqueur, if using.
4 Leave both mixtures to cool and thicken, stirring occasionally. Whisk the egg whites until soft peaks form. Fold half into each mixture.
5 Place alternate spoonfuls of light and dark mixtures into glass sundae dishes, stirring as you go with a thin skewer to create a marbling effect.
6 Scrape the thin edge of the chocolate bar with a vegetable peeler to make curls and use to decorate the mousses. Serve with crisp dessert biscuits. *Serves 6.*

Bread, Butter & Brandy Pudding

A luxurious variation of a popular traditional pudding. Serve with thick set yogurt or whipped cream.

75g (3oz) raisins
grated rind and juice of
1 orange
3 tablespoons brandy
6 slices wholemeal bread,
crusts removed
softened butter for spreading

60g (2 oz/⅓ cup) light soft
brown sugar, or 2-3 table-
spoons clear honey
2 eggs
470ml (15 fl oz/1¾ cups) milk
good pinch of grated nutmeg
2 teaspoons demerara sugar

1 Put the raisins, orange juice and 1 tablespoon brandy in a bowl. Cover and cook on HIGH for 30 seconds. Set aside to allow the raisins to absorb the juice.

2 Lightly grease a 1 litre (32 fl oz/4 cup) microwave dish. Butter the bread, spreading well to the edges. Cut each slice in half, diagonally.

3 Arrange the bread and raisins in the dish in layers, sprinkling brown sugar in between or trickling over the honey.

4 Beat the eggs, orange rind, milk and nutmeg together, then slowly pour over the pudding. Allow to stand for 30 minutes to make sure the liquid is well absorbed. Sprinkle over the demerara sugar.

5 Cook on HIGH, uncovered, for 5 minutes, then on MEDIUM for a further 5 minutes. Sprinkle with the remaining brandy and serve warm. *Serves 4-6.*

Chocolate Collettes

Sometimes, instead of serving a pudding at the end of a meal, I make a plate of these pretty homemade chocolates and put them out alongside the fruit and cheese. They invariably disappear fast.

125g (4oz) plain (dark)
  chocolate, in pieces
155ml (5 fl oz/⅔ cup) double
  (thick) cream
60g (2 oz) white chocolate, in
  pieces

1 passion fruit
TO DECORATE:
1-2 tablespoons chopped
  pistachio nuts

1 Put the plain (dark) chocolate in a small bowl and melt on HIGH for 2 minutes. Stir until smooth.
2 Using a thin pastry brush, coat the insides of 12 petits fours cases with chocolate and chill until firm. Remelt the remaining chocolate on HIGH for 30 seconds, then add a second coat. (Alternatively, using a teaspoon, spoon the melted chocolate into each cup and work it round the sides with the back of the spoon. This is a more basic method and not quite as neat, but still effective if you are short of time – or a beginner.) Chill until firm, then carefully peel off the paper. Don't worry if the chocolate breaks a little; the truffle mixture will seal it.
3 Melt the white chocolate in a medium bowl on HIGH for 30 seconds, then allow to cool slightly. Whip the cream until soft peaks form and fold in the melted white chocolate.
4 Meanwhile, heat the passion fruit on HIGH for 30 seconds. Roll the fruit a little in your hands; this helps release more juice. Halve, scoop out the pulp and seeds into a small sieve over the cream mixture, then press out as much juice as possible, using a wooden spoon. Discard the seeds. Mix the juice into the cream.
5 Pipe or spoon the truffle cream into the chocolate cases and chill for 30 minutes until set. Sprinkle with chopped pistachios. *Makes about 12.*

Chocolate Fudge Cake

If your microwave has a turntable, you may find the cake rises slightly more on one side because of the swirling as it turns. Serve with tea or coffee, or topped with lightly whipped cream as a wickedly rich dessert.

155g (5oz/1¼ cups) self-raising
flour
30g (1oz/¼ cup) cocoa powder
pinch of salt
90g (3oz/⅓ cup) caster sugar
60g (2oz/⅓ cup) dark soft
brown sugar
125ml (4 fl oz/½ cup) milk
60g (2oz) butter, cut into pieces

few drops of vanilla essence
2 eggs, beaten lightly
ICING:
185g (6oz/1 cup) icing sugar
2 tablespoons cocoa powder
60g (2oz) butter
2 tablespoons hot water
few drops of vanilla essence
pinch of salt

1 Sift the flour, cocoa powder, salt and caster sugar into a large bowl or food processor.
2 Put the brown sugar, milk, butter and vanilla essence into a microwave jug and cook on HIGH for 1 minute or until melted. Stir well to blend.
3 Pour onto the dry ingredients, with the eggs, and beat well until smooth. Pour into a greased 20cm (8 inch) microwave-proof ring mould.
4 Cook on HIGH for 5 minutes, turning half-way through. Stand for 10 minutes, then turn out onto a wire rack.
5 When the cake is cool, cut into 2 layers. To make the icing, sift the icing sugar and cocoa powder into a mixing bowl. Put the other ingredients into a jug and heat on HIGH for 1½ minutes. Add to the icing sugar and beat until smooth. Allow to cool a little.
6 Sandwich the cake together with a little of the icing. Slowly pour the rest of the icing over the cake to coat evenly. Allow to set, then carefully transfer to a serving plate.
Serves 6-8.

Carrot Ring Cake

Cakes baked in the microwave can look pale and unappetising, so I choose ingredients that are already well coloured, like the carrots in this recipe.

185g (6oz/1½ cups) self-raising
   flour
½ teaspoon bicarbonate of soda
¼ teaspoon ground cinnamon
125g (4oz/¾ cup) light soft
   brown sugar
185g (6oz) carrots, peeled and
   finely grated
2 eggs
125ml (4 fl oz/½ cup)
   sunflower oil
grated rind and juice of
   1 orange

60g (2oz/½ cup) chopped
   walnuts
60g (2oz/⅓ cup) sultanas
   or raisins
ICING:
90g (3oz/⅓ cup) cream cheese,
   softened
2 tablespoons icing sugar, sifted
few drops of vanilla essence
TO DECORATE:
walnut halves and carrot
   shreds (optional)

1 If necessary, lightly grease a 20cm (8 inch) microwave-proof ring mould. (Some moulds do not require greasing.)

2 Sift the flour, bicarbonate of soda and cinnamon together into a large mixing bowl. Mix in the sugar and grated carrot.

3 Beat together the eggs, oil and orange juice, then mix in to the dry ingredients, beating well. Fold in the orange rind, walnuts and dried fruit.

4 Pour the mixture into the mould and level the surface, tapping the mould gently to exclude any air pockets. Stand on an upturned sauce or plate in the microwave and cook on HIGH for 6-7 minutes, until the cake has risen and is firm to touch.

5 Leave to stand for 10 minutes, then turn out onto a wire rack to cool completely.

6 Place all the icing ingredients in a bowl and mix until smooth, then spread evenly over the cake, swirling the icing attractively. Decorate the top with walnut halves and carrot shreds. *Serves 6-8.*

Apricot & Almond Jam

Homemade apricot jam, using the concentrated flavour of dried fruit, is gorgeous. This is a much easier method than jam-making in the conventional way in a preserving pan. Use the kind of dried apricots which do not need soaking. It is important to use a deep microwave bowl for this, or the mixture will bubble up.

250g (8oz/1¾ cups) dried apricots, chopped
4 tablespoons lemon juice
470ml (15 fl oz/1¾ cups) boiling water

500g (1lb) granulated sugar
60g (2oz/¼ cup) flaked almonds
2 tablespoons Grand Marnier (optional but nice)

1 Put the apricots, lemon juice and boiling water in a large bowl. Cover and cook on HIGH for 15 minutes, stirring twice.
2 Add the sugar and cook on HIGH for 2 minutes. Stir well. If any sugar crystals remain, cook for a further 1 minute; it is important that every crystal is dissolved.
3 Cook on HIGH for 10 minutes until setting point is reached. To test for setting, spoon a small amount onto a chilled saucer. Wait a few minutes, then push the jam away from you with your finger. If a skin forms and wrinkles, setting point has been reached. If not, then cook for a further 2-5 minutes. Stir two or three times during cooking.
4 Leave to stand for 5 minutes, then stir in the almonds and liqueur. Pour into warm, clean, sterilized jars. Cover, seal and label. *Makes 1kg (2lb)*.

Index